Neither is the Horse
and
Other Poems

Neither is the Horse
and
Other Poems

Rory Motion

CASSELL&CO

First published in the United Kingdom in 2001 by Cassell & Co

Text and illustrations copyright © Rory Motion 2001

Design and layout copyright © Cassell & Co 2001

Photographs © Cassell & Co 2001

A CIP catalogue record for this book is available from the British Library

ISBN 0-3043-6241-7

Photography by Rachael Evans

Design by Bess Frimodig

Editor John Mitchinson

Typeset in Gill Sans

Printed and bound in Great Britain by MPG Books Ltd, Bodmin, Cornwall

Cassell & Co

Orion House

5 Upper St Martin's Lane

London WC2H 9EA

I would like to dedicate this book of poems to Huddersfield Town A.F.C. without whom the football league would be without one of its teams.

I'm a Hippie

I believe in angels and reincarnation
I believe the pyramids contain coded information
I believe imagination is the true source of wealth
I believe in glasses from the National Health

I believe in the benefits of retaining vital fluids
I believe Ken Barlow in real life's a druid
I believe that Jesus sometimes liked a joke
I like to think that Prince Charles has probably had a toke

I believe in the lost continents of Atlantis and Mu
I believe in tahini, tai chi and tofu
I believe there's a secret language in the stones
I believe in infinity and wholemeal scones

I believe in gnostics, josticks and karma
I believe in Captain Beefheart and the Dalai Lama
I believe bees come from outer space
I like to think that kindness could save the human race

I believe it is below as it is above
I believe Glastonbury in real life's a dove
I believe in flapjacks and fingerless gloves
I believe in bare feet, barleycup* and Love

*Barleycup is a coffee, nay, a pleasure substitute. "Ba-li-cup" is a Polish word
which translates directly as "instant brown drink". The only way to get
a narcotic hit off it is to sprinkle it onto an Aqua Libra slammer.

Uncle

One day my fourteen year old niece said to me
"Uncle Rory, are you a hippie?"
"What makes you say that?" I asked
"Because you live in mid-Wales," she said
"And wear little round glasses
And jumpers with wildlife on
And sometimes
You're indecisive
and smell of stale biscuits."

Bible

I've never read the Bible
But I've seen the film with Charlton Heston
There was one with Robert Powell
But Charlton's was the best 'un

National Identity and the Male Psyche

My penis grows small
Every time England lose at Football
For our '93 World Cup failure
I thank Graham Taylor
He shrank my genitalia
We paid for our total lack of finish
It made my scrotal sac diminish

Art

When I was a kid

David Hockney used to come around to our house

And play Subbuteo with my dad

And from those days

I used to have a David Hockney original

which would be worth thousands now

If I still had it

The problem was that it was on Etch-a-Sketch

Because of the fingertip control that David had got

(From playing Subbuteo so much with my dad)

He could do the curve of buttocks and

Light reflecting from swimming pools

Whereas all I could do

Was a Manhattan sky line

Although sometimes I'd draw a dead straight line on it

And show it to my dad

Who was recovering from heart surgery

Mut!

I'm not a top dog breeder; I'm an actor

With a chunky pullover

And a firm and meaty voice

And I recommend you to purchase Mut!

When you shake it out of the tin

It makes a ch ch ch sound

And looks like a cylindrical jobbie on the plate

Mut! Looks and smells so totally repellant

That you'll be really glad your dog's eating it

And not you .... So purchase Mut!

And get your dog around that

Pal

Ode to Swampy

And did those feet in ancient Doc Martens
Walk beneath England's mountains green
And was the hole he dug quite long
Under England's pleasant pastures unseen

And did his countenance begrimed
Shine forth on "Have I got news for you"
And was the A30 still builded there
By England's dark satanic 'out of town' shopping centres

Bring me my blow and Golden Virginia
Bring me my Rizlas of desire
Bring me my Spear and Jackson, oh clods unfold
Bring me a torch, three blankets, a good book and a flask
of barley cup

I will not cease from environmental strife
Nor shall my spade sleep in my hand
Till we have stopped building these polyester nightmare jungles
Where the mute howl of frozen fish finger agony
Pierces the groaning slabs of retail nothingness
In England's green and pleasant land

Frank

This is the land that Frank Worthington trod

This is the grass and that is the sod

That on the first Saturday of sixty nine

In the last minute of extra time

Held Frank's toes

As his left leg rose

To crack in a stormer

(top left hand corner)

New from Meatcleaver Brothers

Spaghetti Entrails
Delicious pieces of pasta
Shaped into all the major internal
Organs of the body
In a rich realistic tomato sauce
They're fun! They're educational!
You can practice spare part surgery
On the comfort of your own toast
With Spaghetti Entrails
They can turn a snack
Into a bloodbath

Bicycle

Somewhere out on the York bypass
Underneath a bomber's moon
Was a four-door Ford wild west saloon
Driven by an F-registered executive baboon
Who overtook the undertaker
And pulled out too soon
And I rode on my bike through the mud
And said four wheels bad two wheels good
I really love my bicycle she makes me feel inspired
Her little wheels go round and round
Even though they're under pressure and tired

He could feel the soft urgent grip of his cycle clips
sending hot spasms of pleasure thrilling through his thrashing
body. Firm fingers found and clicked the willing Sturmey
Archer. Twenty-five kilos of bad-ass Raleigh Europa surged into
the hot York night

I've got lead free legs for you
I love you more with every bump
I love the way your sweet pedals fall
I love the way you wear your pump

Bootham Bar was like an anus, each car a shiny bolus of food
passing in slow peristalsis through the intestinal labyrinth of the
York one-way system and when the traffic lights changed it was
like a huge bowel motion, each car a shiny turd
accelerating towards Easingwold and infinity

I really love my bicycle
She's all I need to get around
Airplanes are much faster
But they're no good around town
(I can handle bars and cycle paths
I can't handle cars and psychopaths)

Country Song

If you can't come back tomorrow please come back today
Another sunrise means sorrow since you went away
From the time you said goodbye and the darkness fell too soon
I've been floating by in an empty sky and lonely as the moon

You were the one that made the wound,
    the one that made me wise
You made me play a different tune, you made me realise
I was getting high and saying hi to the people in the room
But I was floating by in an empty sky as lonely as the moon

Now I'm a one-man band again and I'm bound to write a song
Try and understand the pain and try to right a wrong
Find some easy words to say and play a simple tune
As I float on by in an empty sky as lonely as the moon

I pray to genius and boldness as I travel through the land
Come home late to coldness from a one night stand
I sit down and I sigh in my "this ain't livin" room
As I float on by in an empty sky as lonely as the moon

And I'm the lone ranger; I've got Silver on my back
I'm the imperfect stranger you might meet me on the track
I can't fix the crack of dawn or mend the break of day
And no-one mends a broken heart
    they were meant to be that way

Easter

It was Easter
And I wanted to take advantage
Of the prevailing spiritual impulse
And find a way to resonate
With the suffering and passion
Of Christ on the cross
So I accepted a gig in Blackpool

The sun was shining and the sea sparkled
With a million radioactive turds
The golden mile was just a front
I was playing the central pier
On the North pier was Ray "Chubby" Brown
And on the South pier
Was Jim "Sad Bastard" Davidson
There was a lot of pier pressure

War

Scuds scud like only a good scud could
A bit like a patriot missile but not as good
A patriot missile whistles stars and stripes
And all the boys eat apple pies
And smart bombs are smart
But they're not wise

Dallas Ethiopia

I'm Dallas Ethiopia of TV and Radio fame

Read about me in your Newspaper I'll be next to the bingo game

And if things don't change they'll stay the same

I'm Dallas Ethiopia, the man with no middle name

My body's just bones stretched with skin

I paid a surgeon ten thousand dollars to put a Kirk Douglas dimple
on my chin

I like the bit in the Bible best

When Jesus gets it off his chest

And turns over the tables in the stock exchange

I'm Dallas Ethiopia, the man with no middle name

A boatful of dead sheep from New Zealand was sailing by with
its load

Past the empty horn of Ethiopia to the co-op on the Halifax road

I'm dying to be wild but I was born to be tame

I'm Dallas Ethiopia, the man with no middle name

Union

A trade union is the third best union to be had
Mystical union is best of all
And sexual union's not bad

Inky Clumps

With my Bic biro spade
On the papers flat white virgin belly
I planted you a quick growing Black Forest of lies
Each letter was a tree
Growing on the parallel horizons of the page
Words lurked like inky clumps
Each one a glyph
Mysterious in meaning and richer than the shadows
Yes
Glyph richer than the shadows
We're all going on a summer holiday
No more worries for a week or two
Cliff knicked a quiff and a riff From Billy Fury
Got sent down by Juke Box Jury
Thought they were gonna send him down for life
But Janice was the judge she said I'll give him five

Let your reading eyes pulverize

The Black Forest of lies

And the magic mill of your mind

Pulp the inky clumps

Then from the heavenly rollers of your heart

Let steam fresh reams

Of new paper dreams

And when we are ready

And the dreamers are singing

Yes

Ready and the dreamers

Are singing

You were made for me

Everybody tells me so

You were made for me

Don't tell me that you don't know

Mrs Donkersley's Chutney

The local transport in Yorkshire is very friendly
I catch the bus in Holtby on its way from Pocklington to York
via Stamford Bridge
And I always take fresh produce from the garden
To swap with the other passengers
Sometimes we build a fire in the aisle
And sing songs
Or tell stories about the creation myths of Pocklington and
Stamford Bridge
On the back seat there is always Mrs Donkersley
And even though she's in her late seventies
She's still really interested in Tantric sex
Often she'll say "Hey! Rory!
Come and plant your magic lollipop tree in my jade garden
    of desire!"
And I know that if I do
She'll give me a jar of her homemade Victoria plum chutney
And this plum chutney is absolutely fantastic
You take just a small mouthful
And suddenly you're plunged headlong
Into a swirling ocean of sensual bliss
And you haven't got a clue what's going on
But soon you learn to ride
The outrageous surf of pleasure
And you begin to realise
That individual flavours
Single celebrations of each specific spice
Are arriving on crested waves
(which obviously break in spumes of ecstasy
on the shorelines of your consciousness)

And the distance between these waves
Are the very intervals of magic
Divine ratios from sacred mathematics
Describing the growth curves of the universe
And long after the physical taste of the
Chutney is gone
These subtle patterns inform and instruct
Your sub-atomic particles
So that your whole body
Feels like a choir-filled cathedral
And your soul is a chorister
In the soaring hymn to eternal joy

And it's got raisins in

Sherlock Holmes I

Sherlock Holmes was having breakfast

He couldn't wait to investigate

His enquiring mind compelled him to find

What's on Watson's plate

Sherlock Holmes discovered most

While employing subtle means

So first of all he grilled the toast

But wouldn't spill the beans

He held the knife for questioning

He tried to pin down the fork

The milk nearly lost its bottle

The Rice Krispies wouldn't talk

He saw a saucer flying

To the defence of an innocent cup

The table cloth was lying

It was definitely covering up

Sherlock Holmes was getting nowhere

And the time was getting late

He was no was nearer to the answer

To "What's on Watson's pate?"

Meanwhile Watson had finished breakfast

The contents of his plate had gone from view

And so being a dutiful assistant

He gave Sherlock Holmes a clue

He drew a line from his throat to his belly

And said, "What's the name of this canal?"

"Alimentary, my dear Watson"

said Sherlock to his pal

Larissa

Army surplus, King's Cross madonna
Flame haired Isis of the Marylebone Road
Know that I am wounded!
Huge beacons of hope blazed with fierce anticipation
On the high mountain tops of my heart
Whilst in some obscure damp valley of thine
A small candle briefly flickered
Before I phoned you from the station
My eyes were two shining lakes
Smiling in a valley landscape of love and pure grace
That same valley, now flooded with tears
Is a reservoir and there is no life
In the drowned village of my sunken face
However
Deep inside the dark hills of my disappointment
I have mined every vein
For the precious ore of consolation
Melted it in the white hot furnace of my desire
Moulded it in reason's womb
And upon the anvil of my soul
Hammered, shaped and honed it
Into a glistening sword of unconditional forgiveness
Let the shining blade of that sword
Sever the tawdry knots of past mistakes
And in some sweet and as yet unwritten future
Let us walk unburdened
Through the afternoon art galleries
Of London's sovereign streets

Merry Business

Cash registers in chorus ring
Glory to the newborn king
The tree is cut, the cake is iced
Time and turkey sacrificed
Backseat neon angels nod
Whisper happy birthday, God
Electro megadeath he-men ping
Microwaving turkeys ding
Hark the triumph herald sings

Love and frozen peas on earth
A plastic star proclaims the birth
The truth of ages is revealed
Christ was born in Huddersfield
Mary was ready but the shops were shut
So Christ was born in a Pizza Hut
The three wise shoppers came by car
And left their gifts by the salad bar
And the angel of the lord came down
And ate sweetcorn

Sentimental breakdown trucks
Loaded up with bambi books
Donald ducks and dives for cover
Merry business, big brother
Santa's claws are sharp this year
He drives a V12 reindeer
Dallas Disney Dickens fuse
TV Jesus on the news
Off white Christmas
Off white blues

Sherlock Holmes II

Sherlock Holmes was sculpting
A bust upon the beach
Always using something
Just within his reach

Pretty soon the bust
Was looking jolly groovy
Using as he does
Only objets trouvé

The whole thing made entirely
Of flotsam and jetsam
And when he doesn't find any
He gets Watson to get some

I was a Stuntman for Ken Barlow

I worked unseen behind the scenes
Of *Coronation Street*
I rolled up Ray Langton's sleeves
And fed the cat that roamed
The shining rooves
Wet with northern rain
Stan Ogden was my long-lost brother
I was Elsie Tanner's first lover
Ena Sharples was my earth mother

Jolly Tom Waits Afternoon

The captain sailor's mother's drunk in a sad café down by the
docks
She's dancing with a one-armed dwarf with cocaine in his socks
And the Chinaman's in the corner, he's drinking whiskey and
blood
Smiles razors at the mirror all his teeth are made of wood
And the hotel's made of nicotine and ice
And the captain lost his mother playing dice

The piano player's only got one eye, sees his doctor once a
week
His mouth made of plasticine melts open when he speaks
And upstairs in a hotel room in number two six four
Ted the gambler and the Chinaman are doing yoga on the floor
And down the hall the boys are snorting iron ore
Ted the gambler says that he can take some more

Mr Priest is asking questions though he says that he knows it all
And everyone starts speaking Spanish when you pass them in
the hall
And the piano player's stopped playing now he's got something
in his eye
And outside the wind is howling and a baby starts to cry
And the whole moon is made of cherry pie
And the Chinaman never wears a tie

The desk clerk's name is Romeo, plays a scarlet saxophone
His mouth is like a graveyard all his teeth are made of stone
And checkout time is 10am but the taxi's got bald tyres
And Romeo keeps spitting on his hands all his fingernails on fire
And the nighthawks are talking down the wire
And the Chinaman says he's not for hire

All his cigarettes are bleeding and his heart is on parole
There's a Portuguese couple getting hot and his coffee's getting cold
And the French girl in the blue dress, the one that broke his spine
She pinched his best friend's watch chain and now she's doing time
And she's waiting for the night train heading south
There's a funeral going on inside his mouth

She said she'd be his valentine and kiss his snake tattoo
She got married to a gypsy man with jewels from Peru
And all the lights start going out and the street begins to sweat
And Romeo says he knows where it's at but he hasn't told her yet
And the walls are dripping cheap perfume
And Juliet walks across the room
And says it's another jolly Tom Waits afternoon

Caps Off

I was watching the match at Leeds Road
It started raining
The two old blokes in the next seats
Took their caps off
"Excuse me," I said
"Why are you taking your caps off?"
"Nay, lad," the nearest one replied
"I'm not going to sit all night
In a damp cap."

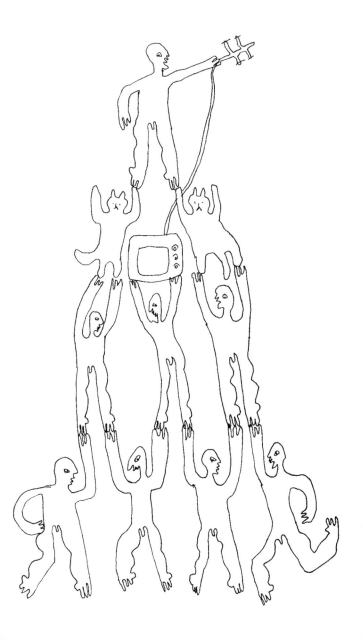

Viking Song

Every winter we get snowed in
Even though we pray to Odin
So we set sail in the blizzards and the gales
In our long johns in our longships
We don't mind the long trips
To England for the January sales

We find it cuts down on the labour
To take the cross channel saver
It's a shame the lads get funny out to sea
By the time we reach the border
They're completely out of order
In their struggle to get the duty free

And I'm sorry for invading your country
As Vikings that's how we get along
Try not to think of it as an invasion
It was just a shopping trip that went wrong

There's nothing more exciting
To a well-adjusted Viking
Than a plate of turnips followed by some pillage
And it's nice to dress up weird
And put goose fat on your beard
And have some fun laying waste a village

We like to drink strong lagers
And tell each other dirty sagas
Life as a Viking can be hard
We have to do our shopping overseas
'Cos we haven't got a Sainsbury's

And nobody accepts my Barclaycard
(A huge horned helmet and a massive big axe!
That'll do nicely, Sir!)

And I'm sorry for invading your country
As Vikings that's how we get along
Even though it's cold in Scandinavia
It's no excuse for my behaviour
It was just a shopping trip that went wrong

Spring

Vile sick stench
Breath of liars
Bile will quench
The beltane fires
Vernal infection
The daisies curse
General election
May the first

Escape

I was in the kitchen in my dressing gown
Waiting for the knowledge of a lost civilization
To snake a caravan of truth
Across this blasted desert of sleep
I was looking out of the window
At the impossible green fire of sunset
And as it faded into a deep dark
Foreboding red
And the very earth seemed to bruise
Under the fall of suffocating night
I thought to myself
I think I'll have a cup of tea
And watch the telly

Albert and the Rave

There's a famous hippy festival called Glastonbury
Noted for its fresh air and fun
And Mr & Mrs Ramsbottom
Went there with young Albert their son

A grand little punk was young Albert
All dressed in his best quite a swell
He had some skunk that he couldn't really handle
The finest the dealers could sell

He didn't think much to the Craft field
The crowds was all fiddling and small
They were all relaxed and mellow and grounded
In fact nothing to freak out at all

So seeking further amusement
He took an E and went to a rave
Where they all sweated profusely
And said "wicked" and "sorted" and "safe"

There was one great big DJ called Wallace
Who played techno and jungle and rap
And they all thought it was groovy
Except young Albert, who thought it was crap

So straightaway brave little feller
Not showing a morsel of fear
Toked on the skunk that he couldn't really handle
And shouted in Wallace's ear

My name is Albert Ramsbottom
And I'm just down for the day
And I was wondering if you could play some Temptations
Four Tops or Marvin Gaye

You could see the DJ didn't like the idea
For giving a kind of a grin
He put on some ultra-hard techno jungle
Which did the little lad in

Now Pa who had seen the occurrence
And didn't know what to do next
Said "Ma, yon DJ's freaked out our Albert,"
And Ma said, "Ee, I am vexed."

Then Mr and Mrs Ramsbottom
Quite rightly when all's said and done
Complained to the rave organiser
That the DJ had freaked out their son

Now Ma, who had turned a bit awkward
When she thought how her son's mind had gone
Said "NO! someone's got to be summoned,"
So that was decided upon

So off they went to the Healing Field
Where the wise woman was hanging about
And they explained what had happened to Albert
And about the DJ freaking him out

The wise woman gave her opinion
That the techno was really to blame
And what with the E and the skunk
Well, it had scrambled the little lad's brain

So she gave him a joint of some homegrown
And made him lie in a field
And she put on a Van Morrison tape
And soon young Albert was healed

At that Ma got proper grateful
"Well, thank you miss," said she
And she had a quick toke on the homegrown
And they all went home for their tea

Christmas

In the video of Christmas there should be a pause
Where we ought to spare a thought for poor old Santa Claus
While we recline and dine and just enjoy ourselves
Santa's working overtime in the North Pole with his elves

Never slacking Santa slaves no chance to watch the box
He's busy packing aftershave and underpants and socks
He can't relax in any way, he's got to go full speed
He's got to tax the sleigh and get the reindeer MOT'd

He's got to navigate the globe and fill a billion stockings
Wishing he was back at home watching *Mary Poppins*
But he's got to go to Wilmslow and then to Khatmandu
Then Bolivia back to Bolton, calling in at Crewe

We always leave him sherry and three or four mince pies
That's why Santa's always merry and rather oversize
But Santa never drinks and drives, he puts the sherry in his sack
And gets blotto in the grotto with the elves when he gets back

Goal!

A cross came in from the corner
Not to score was surely a sin
St John smote the woodwork
And Jesus hammered it in

Andy Booth

The pulsating pushing animal passion
Of Goodman and Bull was spent
The futile semen of their crude caress
Dried harmlessly on the soft green edge
Of the six yard box
And then it happened
The once mighty swelling sea of
Surging black and gold desire
Was suddenly millpond still and silent
And looking out onto the hard grey green grass
Of Kilner Bank
Their empty eyes mirrored the hollow dullness
Of the sad November sky
High above a seagull wheeled and cried
And echoing in the cavernous void
Of their shattered minds
The wind whispered
Booth-ee! Booth-ee!

Pheasant

Although bred for murder
This pheasant had style
So we stopped and talked
About life for a while
Besides insect nutrition
His overriding ambition
Was to shit on the Duke of Argyll

My Dad

My Dad believed that Geoffrey Boycott
Was an advanced soul from Atlantis
Who came out of the sea off Bridlington
On a golden chariot
Pulled by seven golden whippets
And made his way to Guiseley
The home of Harry Ramsden's fish'n'chip shop

    Hari Ramsden Hari Ramsden
    Hari Hari Ramsden Ramsden

My Dad believed that fish and chips
Were deeply symbolic
He said that the fish represented the Piscean Age
And that the chips
Were to fill you up

My Dad believed in Yorkshire ley lines
He says if you join up cricket pitches, pubs
And ancient fish and chip shops
They form these mysterious alignments
Across the landscape

My Dad believes that when you die
You go to *Emmerdale Farm*
My Dad was one of the first hippies in Yorkshire
He had flared clogs
He was in a band and played a coal-fired
Fender Doncaster
Which they had to stoke up on solos

My Dad once hitch-hiked from Hull to Liverpool
With his mate Jack Barraclough
And wrote a seminal book called *On t'Road*

My Dad smokes coal
If he's got a big lump of black he's happy
I'll say to him, "Hey, Dad, this stuff's rubbish
It doesn't crumble very well
And you have to put a lot in"
And he'll say,
"I know it's rubbish, son
But it's only eighty quid a ton"

Dit Oui

La France aux Anglais

L'Angleterre aux Français

Les Etats Unis aux Bulgars

L'Italie aux Hongois

La Suisse aux Mexicans

L'Autriche aux Africans

Le Thibet aux Belges

La Senegal aux Danois

Le Pays de Gaulles aux Chinois

L'Allemagne aux Hollandais

L'Espagne aux Portugais

L'Haute Loire aux Charentais

La Cote d'Ivoire aux Japonais

Le Thibet aux Belges

Oh Jean Marie just dit Oui!

Dit n'importe ou aux n'importe Qui

Carnival

Ladbroke Grove is funkier than York
In York you see policemen walking
On the beat
But in Ladbroke Grove
You see them walking
On the off-beat

No Blues Blues

I sat down to sing the blues and everything was fine
Then I found I had a problem, no blues on my mind
I've got the no blues blues, can't think of nothing bad
Got the no blues blues, best thing I've ever had

I want to get down and moan, holler and shout
But every time I start to groan, I find the sun's come out
I've got the no blues blues, can't think of nothing bad
Got the no blues blues, best thing I've ever had

My baby hasn't left me, got no holes in my shoes
My radio is broken so I can't hear the news
I've got the no blues blues, can't think of nothing bad
Got the no blues blues, best thing I've ever had

Cool

Now I saw a cat, dead on the pavement
"Wow! Look at that!" I said in amazement
It wasn't in a pool of red where it died
It looked pretty cool with its head on one side
So I gave it a stroke and straightened its fur
It looked a bit like that bloke Damon from Blur

Dream

A shining night
Without armour
With you

Eric Cantona

Il est un star Eric Cantona

Il est un ange

Il est un melange

Insolite est rare

Il a le tendresse du Mirielle Matthieu

Il est un peu comme Giresse

Il a la poitrine du Gerard Depardieu

Il a la gravité de Monsieur Mitterand

Il a l'assurance et grandeur du Mont Blanc

Il a la charme de Maurice Chevalier

La poesie de Baudelaire

Il est un vrai Francais

Mais il joue en Angleterre

Oui, c'est vrai, pour un moment

Monaco ils avaient Glen Hoddle

Et je sais, pour quelques saisons,

Marseilles ils avaient Chris Waddle

Mais en Angleterre, il y a qu'un Francais

Mais celui la, oui, c'est un vrai

J'ai dit, "Ooh la la la la la la la la

Merci France pour Eric Cantona"

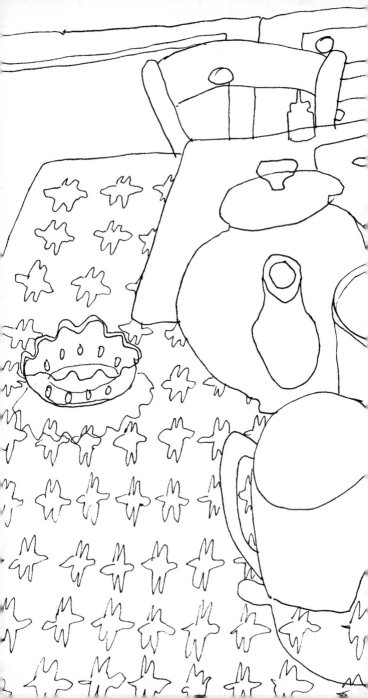

Think

Think globally act locally
Think cosmically act stupidly

Sheep Prefer Landscapes

You jumped up Joe 90

Miserable monochrome

First-class post-nihilist

Self-addressed envelope

Million pound styling

Fashionable hireling

Art establishment jerks

I'd like to talk to you

About your contemptible works

You drown out the best with the rest

And leave us the worst

So there are no surprises

When you say the last one is first

And just when the emperor's wardrobe

Is ready to burst

You go and give prizes

To people like Damien Hirst

Malta

A used pumice stone
In a shallow shared
Blue Bath
Encrusted with the dead skin
Of Africa, Europe and Asia
A piece of grit
In the terrified eye
Of a weeping western world

Housing Benefit

Holding my numbered ticket
I waited so long in the Housing Benefit Office
That I lost the will to live
As I floated out of my body
And saw the waiting long white tunnel
I knew that I was dying
Far below me I could see the minister
And the Neo-Georgian toilets in Parliament Street
Beyond York I could see the fog-sucked fields
Lying flat and listless under a tamazapan sky
And I thought to myself
Except for the library facilities
I'm going to a better place
And I came to that place
Of fields and meadows
And my grandma was waiting for me
With a jumper she'd just knitted
The colours were so intense
They were off the vibrational scale of the planet
(And it fitted underneath the arms)
Then an Angel came and said No!
Your time is not yet
You have work to do on the planet
And I thought, yes
I've got that gig in Leeds on Tuesday
I fell back into my body
And felt again my groaning spirit
Crucified on the cross of matter

Richard Whiteley

I was on *The Richard Whiteley Show*
It could have happened to anybody
Yorkshire Television rang me up and said,
 "Your name's been recommended to us
Could you describe your act?"
I said, "Sure, I'm a shamanic bard
And a mystical troubadour
Whose duty is to hurl mighty words
Of white light and wisdom
Against the demon-controlled structures of the planet"
They said, "Do you want to be on *The Richard Whiteley Show?*"
I said, "Yes, please"

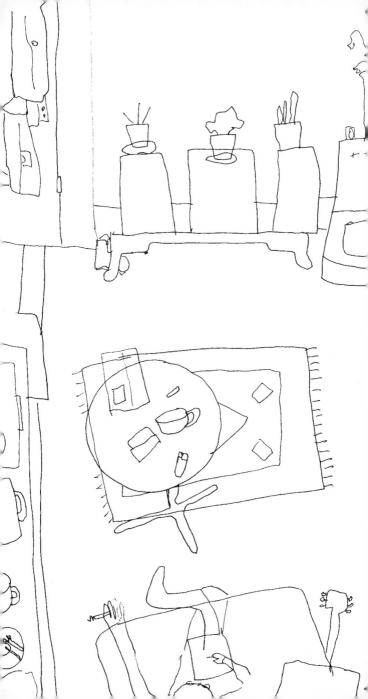

Why TV?

Every time you turn your television on
They come into your room
The all-night alchemists of oblivion
The electronic blacksmiths of doom
Hammering out to airy thinness
Their sad ingot of dross
Give me the big big talent show
With Jonathan Ross

Please burn out my brain
With your unblinking tube of neon nothingness
Render me insane
Fool me into thinking I can't get out of this mess

Zap me with your deadly rays
Sap me with your steady gaze
So the axis of my mind's eye is hypnotized
On your spinning square wheel of death
And the anger that should rise dies
And righteous passion feels no breath
It's inanity unalloyed
It's insanity the neon void
A million brain cells get destroyed
Every time you see Emma Freud
Noel Edmonds is a haemorrhoid
"What's that?" I hear you say
"But you went on *The Richard Whiteley Show*!"
"Ah well, yes," I say
"But I did not lightly go
Into that afternoon of endless night
I raged against the dying light"

"Ostensibly it was to pay my rent
but sadly all the money was spent
On the booze and half an ounce of blow
It took to get through *The Richard Whiteley Show*
(I've learnt to know what luck's worth,
I'm the last one scared to die
I've worked with Vera Duckworth
And the fat one from *Hi-de-Hi*")

Little and Large

In May 1946 Mahatma Ghandi visited London
And Winston Churchill went to visit him
In his hotel room
Ghandi-ji prepared for them both
A simple dish of rice porridge
"The porridge is very lumpy, Mr Ghandi"
Said Winston Churchill
As quick as a flash
The Mahatma turned to Churchill
And said,
"My commitment is to truth
Not consistency."

Les

Les anges

Les avions

Les étoiles

Les Dawson

Free

Free art from artists
Free thought from thinkers
Free spirit from matter
Free beer for drinkers
Free with every breath
Free with every packet
A plastic deep sea diver
That you used to get free in packets of cornflakes

Free jazz from Parkhurst
Free form from colour
Free Nelson Mandela
Free Women
Free as the wind
And the sky and the deep sea
Plastic diver
That used to sink to the bottom of the bottle - ottle - ottle

I was born free and I run free
I'm a free man, Hardy and Willis
And I wouldn't do anything I didn't want to do
I wouldn't go to war for my free shilling
And the plastic diver would come back to the top of the
Bottle - ottle - ottle

Free souls for boots
Free gifts on parachutes
Free falling from the sky
Free market forces
Freely fluctuating
It's a free for all in there

Do you wonder why
Life goes up and down like a plastic deep sea diver?
Thirty seven different types of margarine
Twelve assorted things to keep the kitchen clean
Do you ever wonder if you try too hard to be free?
Free parking for your free Rolls Royce
Free love and free choice
But it doesn't look much like freedom to me
More like a plastic deep sea diver running out of
Baking powder

Free with every breath
Free with every packet
A plastic deep sea diver

Le Tunnel d'Amour

Il y'a un rendezvous dans l'air
Entre la France et l'Angleterre
Et sous la boue et sous la mer
Il y'a un trou extraordinaire
C'est la belle nouvelle ouverture
On l'appelle le tunnel d'amour

Let's get pally, why don't you come over?
I could be Calais, you could be Dover
With the mud down below and the channel up above
We could say "Hello" in the tunnel of love

Lonesome Frozen Turkey

This is a sad song
About a turkey that had a hard life
And had a dream like shining star
That one day he would be eaten with joy, reverence, love
And cranberry sauce
And take part with us on this great journey of life
And in the busy days before Christmas
As many people passed the frozen meat section
He would puff his little chest out
Tight against his designer cling-film jacket
And try and look as plump and oven-fresh as possible
But the people passed him by
And on Christmas Eve
The doors of the supermarket closed forever
And that turkey never made that Christmas plate
He was too late
And I know this story, Ladies and Gentlemen
Because ... I was that turkey

I'm a lonesome frozen turkey
I'm in the fridge all alone
It's Boxing Day and I ain't been sold,
Nobody took me home
I'm a talking turkey talking turkey talk

I'm a lonesome frozen turkey
And my life seems such a waste
My past is one of pain and prison
And my future looks like turkey paste
I'm a talking turkey talking turkey talk

I was born in a ghetto down in Norfolk
so many you couldn't fit us in
I heard my Mama was really bootiful
I heard my Daddy was nothing but a syringe
(How was it for you, dear?)
I'm a talking turkey talking turkey talk

I can hear those frozen peas moaning
I can hear those pork pies howl
And it wasn't Hamlet's uncle, it was Bernard Matthews
Who did murder most fowl
I'm a talking turkey talking turkey talk

And I said, "Hey, mama,
Can this really be the end
To be stuck inside a fridge freezer at Tescos
With only a frozen fish finger for my friend?"
I'm a talking turkey talking turkey talk

Michael Jackson

Oh, mutant kin of unknown race
With unreal skin and melted face
Your latest dance I cannot watch
I hate it when you grab your crotch

Sexy

He was a sexy bus driver
He drove buses wild

Shoot

Leaning from the windows
Reeling it in
Scene down below
They're dealing in sin
Man dressed in red
With a boot full of meat
Got a film in my head
And I'm shooting the street

No time for dinner
No time to reload
I'm watching all the sinners
On the All Saints Road

There's a man dressed in black
On his back on the street
Says he wants his money back
From the man that sold him meat
They can't find his brain
They don't know what he's on
His mind and the last train
Home has gone

The carnival is over
It's all been blown
I'm watching all the sinners
On the All Saints Road

I Sing the Body Electorate

Love by birthright is pre-selected
My House of Lords by my heart is led
All thoughts by experience elected
A House of Commons sits in my head
Thus my constitution makes its choice
And I am self-government complete
I allow royal images to be my voice
And my groin is a marginal seat

Cows

Knee deep in darkness
And the warm ferment
Of their ever-increasing
Excrement

Every dream of death
Stirs the gloomy haze
The foetid steam of breath
Blurs the endless days

And then the shock of release
And the end of dreadful night
Into the fresh green fields
They lurch
Their fat leather bodies
Laughing with light

Fluffy Toy Dog

I had a fluffy toy dog when I was a child

It was supposed to talk

But it wouldn't do its stuff

So I soaked it in petroleum spirit for a while

Put a match to it

And it went woof!

The Sun

I stayed up all night
Thinking about the sun
Then in the morning
It dawned on me

Fish

I did a picture of the Queen Mother
As a train
Coming out of the fireplace
I did another of the Queen
And underneath it I wrote
"This is not the Queen"

I'm a surroyalist

J.C.

Some of my best friends are Jewish
But there's one that's special to me
He's still my buddy though he left his body
In A.D. thirty three
His Dad was big in the cosmos
But he didn't let it go to his head
Right from the start he came from the heart
Which still beats though he's physically dead

Film

The waiters and wanderers

Spent and squandered

Empty-eyed and hungry

Who went to be a star

In a fat movie made of diamonds

But ended up as extras

In a thin film of dirt

The A1

That single symbolic surgical stitch
Whose thin thread
Knits the gaping wound of inequality
From whose sticky crimson occlusion
Pours the precious lifeblood of a nation

Apple Pie

She came to my country farm
Unexpected invitation
She was cool, she was calm
And collected from the station

We tried hard not to touch
She made an apple pie
Nobody said too much
So no one told a lie

We listened to the weather
Storms inside our hearts
We never slept together
We stayed awake far apart

Sweet fool who meant no harm
And had no expectation
She was cool, she was calm
And collected from the station

Mystery

I am empty
I move mysteriously
Nobody knows where I come from
Nobody knows where I'm going
I'm a York bus

Golgotha

And so I said to the assistant,
"Do you sell crucifixes?"
And she said, "Yes …
Do you want a plain one
Or one with a little man on?"

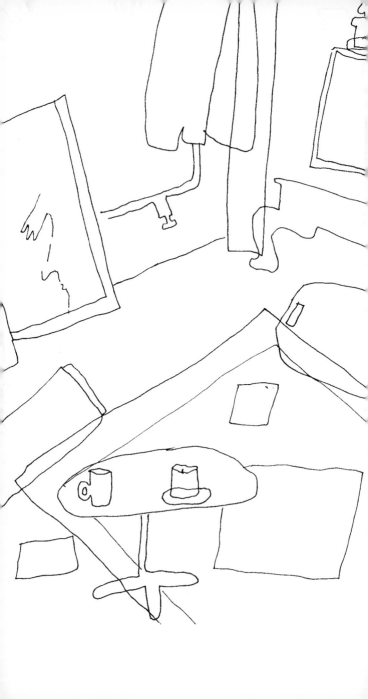

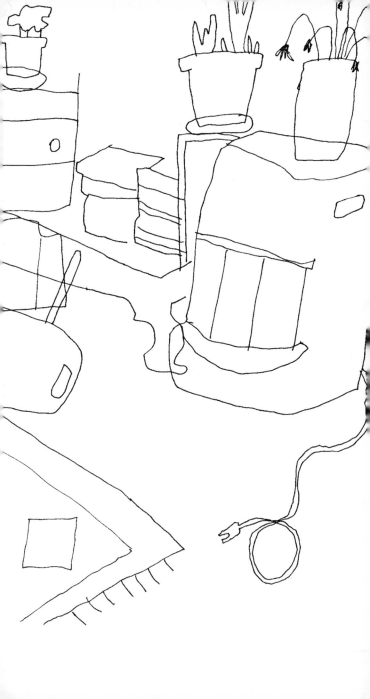

New York New Cops

M I've got a headache.

Captain *There's two Joes face down in the morgue who'd appreciate that headache, Marilyn.*

M I've also got heartache.

Captain *So join the queue, sister – there's not a cop in this city whose heart isn't a piece of raw tender meat rattling in a cage of fear and uncertainty.*

Rod Captain, there's been another murder.

Captain *Where?*

Rod Lower West Side, 25th, white Caucasian chalk circle, 5'10", medium build.

Captain *Let's go.*

M Hold it, I'm coming with you.

Captain *No, it's too dangerous for a dame …*
You've got bosoms.

M But I can sing, listen, "High on a hill was a lonely goatherd …"

Captain *You think I want to go down the Lower West Side 25th and see some guy on the sidewalk with his brains splattered out like a burst melon?*

M Let me come.

Captain *No, you're too tense. Until you learn to see your period as a time of deep transformational power, you'll mess up the whole operation.*

M Don't give me that wise wound crap, Captain. My whole body is roaring red rivers of singing blood.

Captain *There's three Joes face down in the morgue, Marilyn, who'd be glad to have roaring red riv ...*

Rod Captain, there's been another murder ... Upper East Side corner of 23rd and 5th, male, 5'9", white Caucasian chalk circle.

Captain *That's four! It doesn't make any sense.*

M Captain, I think I know who's done this!

Captain *How?*

M Don't ask me how I know. I just know. It's a feeling.

Captain *Dammit, Marilyn, there's four guys face down in the morgue who'd be glad of a feeling. I need some facts, Missy, and you'd better make 'em quick and you'd better make 'em hard!*

M Captain, do you remember when you were a little boy and you'd look at Santa and say, "You are a powerful shamanic figure, who drinks the urine of magic mushroom-eating reindeer and travels between the upper and lower worlds"?

Captain *I remember it like it was yesterday.*

M Well, that man was really your father dressed up and the real Santa is a mythical archetype.

Captain *What are you trying to say, Marilyn, that my father was …*

M Captain, you've got to understand the archetype is always approached but never arrived at.

Rod There's been another murder … Upper Southside, corner of 25th and 4th, male, 5'10", medium build, white Caucasian chalk …

Captain *Cut out the Caucasian chalk circle crap, Rod! There's five Joes face down in the morgue and you just want to …*

M Captain, I think I've started having a baby.

Captain *OK, Marilyn. Don't project your own ideas onto the child too much. Remember that they come through you, they are not of you. Rod, you get some towels and I'll put the kettle on.*

M Captain, you're being marvellous.

Captain *Bullshit, Marilyn, I'm just a guy. You just have this baby and then we'll all go together, me, you and the kid, and nail this hood before he has a chance to …*

Rod Captain, there's been another murder, Lower South East, Upper West Side.

Captain *Not now, Rod. There's a Joe face down in the womb who could use some words of encouragement. Push, Marilyn, push.*

Sporting Life

It's the sporting life and everyone's here
From the landed gentry to the keen-eyed gypsy
They're imbibing wine or drinking beer
They're very drunk or they're slightly tipsy

I met an unstable boy at the bar
Said he worked with horses every day
I asked him if it had affected him so far
But he just shook his head and said, "Nay"

I drank a dram with a drunk from Doncaster
Who said he was happy and glad that he'd been
He'd never known a race run faster
And the whippets were the biggest he'd seen

It's the sporting life and it's good to be knowing
That it doesn't even matter if it rains
'Cos when the going gets soft, the soft get going
Into beer tents to get out of their brains

Racing and drinking seem to be stablemates
It's all to do with Red Rum and chasers
So don't worry if you end up unstable mates
It means you've had a good day at the races

Red Boat

Red Boat, like a packet of Daz

Beneath the billowing flannelette fields

Drying on the washing line horizon

Pegged with trees

God, you've got lovely laundry

A new fresh blue whiteness

And a softness I've never known before

You can digest dirt and stains

That ordinary powers leave behind

High Tea

Whilst on a Nepalese mountain walk
I came across two Yetis
So I took them both back home to York
And we went for tea at Betty's
We ordered toast and tea with lime
And some dainty little ices
And everything was going fine
Till the Yetis saw the prices
They ate two tourists who came from Spain
The way they were was all too horrible
So I never took them there again
Their behaviour was abominable.

It's Over

A poem is a ball that must be delivered
I'm Darren Gough and you're into bat
The fielders of doubt are subtly positioned
I'm running in now … Here it comes … Owzat?

French Afternoon

The dry rattle of sweetcorn leaves
And smooth chevron of geese
Chasing a beaten brass sun
And behind the beat
Of the old bones of summer
I can hear the big bass hum
Of life going on

Recipe for Happiness

Oh Lord, coat my naked forked body
In folds of spicy besan batter
And cast me into the eternal seething wok of love
That I may become the perfect pakora
In a sea of minty yoghurt bliss.

Froggy was a Poet and He did Write, Rimbaud

Poor old Arthur he put down his pen
At the age of eighteen he said, "I'll never write again"
So he took a drunken boat and sailed out to sea
And Arthur never wrote any more sweet poetry.

Sacred Music

Hermes Trimagestus dug Hendrix
Pythagoras was punk
Ghandi liked his indie
While Moses went for funk
Mohammed was a Hank Williams man
Lao Tzu liked Little Feat
Buddha sat around to the Beach Boys sound
Steiner was a Captain Beefheart freak
William Blake played Brit-Pop
Rumi rocked to rap and rave
But Jesus was a soul man
He really liked Sam and Dave

Mid-Wales

Wearing his waistcoat made of old lino stained with the urine of incontinent sheepdogs, Benjamin Jones watched the endless rain. Every three or four years the clouds would break and columns of brown corduroy light would slump against the withering grass. The only time he had left the county was when he had gone with his twin brother Lewis to sell beasts at an auction in Cwmdancing and there they had seen men wearing shoes. That morning he was listening to the farming broadcast as the cat contentedly licked the remains of some ewe's prolapsed uterus from his frayed linen forearms.

Their breakfast consisted of a porcelain bowl of dead pine needles and a small amount of puddle-water poured from an ageing pewter jug. If they wanted something sweet to finish off they would chew small lengths of wind-battered blackthorn root. Afterwards they would read the floral tributes in the *Hereford Times* or go out into the yard to watch the rowanberries thrashing in the gale. If the weather was good they might go out into the fields and play finger-flick football with rabbit droppings.

In the evenings, instead of watching television, they would wait until they got into one of their moods and then watch each other's irises cloud into different densities of grey. Every ten days or so they would have a close relative dying pointlessly in an upstairs bedroom and see how long they could go without expressing any appropriate emotion. Life was never dull in the old farmhouse nestling in the hills above the small village of Llanroverfforwheeldrive.

French Joke

Il y avait deux vaches Anglais qui parle. Une dit a l'autre,
"Tu as entendu du vache fol?", "Oui," dit l'autre, "Mais je
l'attraperai jamais." "Pour quoi pas?" "Parce que je suis
un helicopteur."

Radio 2

From Dawn
(with Tony Orlando)
I listen to Radio 2
All day
Until I'm glad it's night
And the pips

Here's Looking at You

Sun-drunk in the stupid south
I saw a monk with a cupid mouth
Walk at a friendly farmer's pace
I like the Dalai Lama's face

Give Peas a Chance

I'm a mean vegetarian
I buy my flour by the sack
I don't spill my beans for anyone
And I drink my barleycup black
And you pot noodle salesmen
You don't get through my door
I want a fistful of lentils
And a few lentils more

I'm a mean vegetarian
And I don't eat meat
My shoes are made of marmite
That I'm wearing on my feet
I'll eat anything that's wholefood
Anything I can get
But I wouldn't eat the congealed mammary fluids
Of a cow I'd never met

Home

Squeeze of a hallway
Birth of a kitchen
Amniotic comfort of steaming hot tea
The soothing rhythm
Of domestic chit-chat
Cradle of warmth and breast of T.V.

Spear of Destiny

Last summer I went to a car boot sale in Totnes. One of the stalls was a cloth on the ground. It had a few cassettes without boxes, a plastic centrifugal salad dryer, some shrunken t-shirts, a few books (including *The Moon's a Balloon* and *Shardik*) a mini deep-fat fryer, a warped frisbee and, taking up the whole of the top of the sheet, a huge sword that was at least eight feet long.

"What's that?" I said.

"It's the Spear of Destiny" the man replied.

"What's that, then?"

"It's the spear that pierced Christ's side at the crucifixion and afterwards became a magical talisman of reputedly awesome spiritual power, much sought after by warrior priest kings of the next two millenia. It was held by both Charlemagne and Barbarossa. Martel the Hammer repulsed the Moors with it at Poitiers and King Athelstan had it in his possession when he defeated the Danes at the Battle of Malmesbury. Later on it was stolen from the Hapsburg Museum in Vienna by Hitler, who subsequently unleashed unspeakable terrors upon Europe.

Consumed by his own evil Hitler committed suicide and the spear was recovered from an underground bunker in Nuremburg by the liberating American army. In the brief few weeks that the Americans possessed the Spear of Destiny they dropped two atomic bombs on Nagasaki and Hiroshima."

"How much do you want for it?" I asked.

"Twenty quid," he said.

"Would you accept seventeen pounds fifty and throw in the warped frisbee with it?" I asked.

"Sure," he said.

People say to me that in these times of increasing global strife and growing moral uncertainty it must be fabulous to own a magical talisman of such awesome spiritual power and I say, "Yes, it's great, but to be honest I actually have more fun playing with the warped frisbee."

Pigeon Healing

If anybody asks me what sort of people are running this country, I tell them this story:

I was walking by the Houses of Parliament the other day when I noticed a particularly ill-looking pigeon. After a quick inspection I noticed that it had diarrhoea, mite infestation and a bad case of depluming scabies. It also had little warty lumps of necrotic fat hanging from its neck as well as an undershot beak and a mild dose of scaly leg. I did what I could. I bathed its leg in a weak solution of iodine and trimmed its lower mandible. (Any form of surgery on small birds is too expensive, especially when one is working on a small budgie.) I then decided that I ought to give it some spiritual healing. Cupping my hands above its head I blessed it and started work on its crown chakra. A few minutes into the healing and I was concentrating on its heart chakra. I was visualising a warm stream of healing energy passing from the universe through my hands and hopefully into the scarred solar chakra of the pigeon when suddenly I saw the Prime Minister and the cabinet walking towards me. Before I could do anything the Home Secretary ran towards me and punted the pigeon high into the air as though it was a football.

"Stop!" I cried. "That pigeon's got scaly leg and an under-shot beak. I'm giving it spiritual healing, which is very dangerous to interrupt," but they just laughed and carried on playing football with it.

Ladies and gentleman, that's the sort of people who are running this country.

Bob Dylan

Last year I met Bob Dylan in a wholefood shop in Llanfyllin, Mid-Wales. I was buying some joss sticks and I couldn't decide between the frangipani and the honeysuckle and when I looked up, there he was. He was naked from the waist up and was wearing a kilt and a huge black stove-pipe hat and a cheap and obviously fake, stick-on beard. I knew it was him because I could see two faint parallel red marks on his shoulders which could only have been made by years of gentle rubbing from a harmonica harness. I said to him, "Are you Bob Dylan?"

He said, "Well, I guess."

I said, "You look different."

He said, "It's only natural."

I said, "Do you want to go before me?"

He said, "If you want me to, yes!"

Then Mr Price Griffiths Jones walked into the room with a shopping bag in his hand, saw Bob Dylan half-naked and said, "Who is this man?"

I said, "You try so hard but you don't understand exactly what's going on round here. You know something's happening, but you don't know what it is, do you, Mr Price Griffiths Jones?"

Over a cup of tea and a wagon wheel Bob shared a song that he had written during his short stay in Mid-Wales. It was called "Llanrhaeadr-ym-Mochnant (Woman on My Mind)".

Llanrhaeadr-ym-Mochnant (Woman on my Mind)

My sweet angel told me the A490 was best
I was trying to get from Welshpool to Bala in the west
Sweet visions of Llanfyllin and a full moon in my eyes
With my heavy load on the Machynlleth Road
I began to realise
    I had Llanrhaeadr-ym-Mochnant woman on my mind
    She lives in Llanrhaeadr-ym-Mochnant sometimes

My sweet Llanrhaeadr-ym-Mochnant scorpio angel
I will always love you true
Between Oswestry and infinity
I will be with you
And every time we part I'll feel the pain and hurt and sorrow
And your sweet lips will break my heart
When you say, "Tidy yerr, isnit?"
    Llanrhaeadr-ym-Mochnant woman on my mind
    She lives in Llanrhaeadr-ym-Mochnant sometimes

Tiny You Maybe, But You're My Bee

I haven't had a girlfriend for a long time now but last year,
for a few months, I went out with a bee. I met her up at the
local Art college where apparently she was just one of the
gang. The first time I saw her she was entering a marigold.
She was muzzling aside the invaginate folds of the warm
peachy petals and her firm round bottom was vibrating
softly as it explored the sweet mystery of the marigold.
Maybe it was the heat of the day but I realised I was
sexually attracted to this bee and so I asked her out.
Even though the initial impulse to our relationship was
erotic, we didn't actually have sex. When we went
to bed together it was just enough to hold each other.
Obviously there were a few problems. For a start she was
a Libran and I was a Scorpio. However the main problem
was that she was just too small, and not only that, she was
sensitive about it as well. We'd be lying in bed and she'd be
buzzing away in the warmth of my under-arm hair and she'd
say in a sad little voice:
"Rory, do you think I'm too small?" and I would close my
armpit around her reassuringly and say,
"No, for a bee, you're just the right size."
It was beautiful while it lasted but eventually we just drifted
apart. We went for a long walk on a very windy day.

Rites of Passage

In the far corner of Clayton fields
There's a long dark passage to Birkby Hall Road
It's ten feet high and always bending
So you can't see what's coming
Or what's gone behind
And when I go in
I'm nine and I'm frightened
And when I come out
I'm ten and I'm fine
And I've got four fruit salads
And a packet of Swizzles
Which I can get in my mouth
All in one go

Fear of Las Vegas in Lothian

I've always referred to the Edinburgh festival as "the Scottish Festival". Due to the corporate stitch-up I couldn't afford to play in the town centre so I booked a place at venue 666 on the outskirts………
of Carlisle. After the first week the show was cancelled by public demand. The largest audience I ever got was when I got run over by a taxi on Princes Street. I remember a small crowd gathering and shouting things like "Get up, you're crap!"

Ha Ha

The joke is written with a finger on a mirror,
Misted briefly with your own dying breath
Read it and laugh, the punchline's a killer
There's nothing so funny as the paradox of death

Maybe It's Because I'm a Northerner

He-man and Barbie doll
They're such a perfect pair
They're available in London now
And they haven't got any body hair
And they don't smell anywhere
And they drive a dinky GTI.
Get their clothes and food from the ICI
And as they embrace in pulsating polyurethane passion
He-man turns to Barbie doll and says,
"What's a plastic hip-joint like this
Doing in a girl like you?"

Poet Laureate

In April 1999 I received floods of letters congratulating me on being made Poet Laureate. I was flattered indeed that people should think I was worthy of taking the mantle of the laureateship from the powerfully muscular and brooding shoulders of my fellow Yorkshireman, Ted Hughes. I had the fortune to meet him in a small village in Devon a couple of years before he died. He said to me:

"I am the gnat in the ear of the wounded elephant of my own incomprehension," I said, "Fair do's to yer, Ted" (I was only asking him if there was a public telephone nearby).

Pike

Ooh, big fish
Horrid
Sharp teeth
Pointy, pointy
Bitey, bitey
Ow! Ow!

Inner Child

During my stay in Totnes I learnt to access my inner child. Unfortunately, I accessed it whilst I was in the local supermarket and had to slap it on the back of the legs for being stupid.

Compromise

So let's stop fightin'
Let's stop bitchin'
We're always arguing the toss
You call it lichen
I call it lichen
Let's call the whole thing moss

Pantomime

After doing pantomime in Llandudno for three weeks I promised that I would never do it again. I got home and lay on the sofa and cried my eyes out. My girlfriend tried to comfort me. She said, "It's all over now. It's behind you," "Oh no, it isn't!" I replied.

Freud

From the top of a double decker bus in Swiss Cottage
I saw a bust of Sigmund Freud underneath which
somebody had written, "Wanker". From the same bus
a week later I noticed that somebody had erased the
word, "wanker" and written in its place, "My insights
spawned a hideous repression."

I passed it again a week later and somebody had crossed
that out and put, "Wanker".

Freud reckoned the only reason we got out of bed in the
morning was to have sex, whereas Carl Jung gave us the
credit for having a spiritual appetite. I like to think that
Jung's philosophical insights were enriched by his life as a
musician with the band, "Crosby Stills Nash and Jung". (It
was during his time as a drummer with the band that he
wrote his celebrated treatise, *Man and his Cymbals*).

Valentine's Day

Valentine's Day should be your chance to say
Sweet nothings that you normally daren't utter
It should be a chance to start a romance
Take a risk, let your heart have a flutter

L.E.R.V. it's all about lerv
It should be simple but sometimes it's hard
What ought to be magic can turn out to be tragic
For the teenager that doesn't get a card

Kids can be cruel, I remember at school
The day after the postman had come
My friends weren't too tactful, they got cards by the sackful
I got one, out of pity, from my Mum

I felt such a fool, I lost all my cool
It was a terrible thing to go through
I wasn't a hunk, that's what the girls thunk
And 'cos of Valentine's Day everyone knew

It was after that time that things became clear
I became wise in the ways of romance
I got twenty-five Valentines the very next year
I would have had more, but I ran out of stamps

Dennis Law

I had my first full sexual experience at the age of fourteen
when Huddersfield Town got promoted to the
then first division (although I did get an erection when we got
though to the fourth round of the Rumbelows' Cup
the year before). I didn't fall in love, however, until I was
fifteen. (I can't ell you her name because she was Welsh).
At that time my soul was a chocolate pussycat and the heat
of my desire for this woman melted the chocolate pussycat of
my soul and reformed it into a small figurine of Dennis Law.
Ever since that time I've been frightened of falling in love in
case the heat of my desire should damage his soft chocolate
limbs. It gave me an insight into the awesome power of the
human heart and made me realise that supporting
Huddersfield Town was just sex.

Bedsit

The outside of my bedsit
Is painted with skin disease
It could be seborrhoeic dermatitis
Or even psoriasis
The garden's ground elder
Ground glass and rocks
Carpets and syringes
That the junkie threw out of the top window

But I got my friend
To paint outside
His name was Rob
(and he did a good job)
I did some heavy weeding
Now it looks quite nice
And even though my fingernails are bleeding
I've reclaimed a piece of paradise

And the fridge kicks in
Like a war siren
And downstairs
There's the sound of shelling
And the Baby Belling
Is smelling
Of death and rust
And dust devils
Are carpet bombing warplanes of neglect

But I cleaned that room
And I painted it
A very fine shade
Of outer magnolia
I put a carpet down
And now it looks quite nice
And even though my heart is breaking
I've reclaimed a piece of paradise

And the fridge kicks in
Like a war siren
And downstairs
There's the sound of shelling
And the Baby Belling
Is smelling
Of death and rust
And dust devils
Are carpet bombing warplanes of neglect

Wish I Was Here

Set the controls for a hot wash and spin
Set the controls for a hot wash and spin
First get your clothes and then put them in
Set the controls for a hot wash and spin
And welcome
To the washing machine

... careful with that Daz, Eugene ...

... aaaaaaaaaaaaaaaaggggghhhhhhh!

We don't need no fabric softener
We don't need no fabric softener
Hey! ... Washer! ...
Leave those flakes alone!
And welcome
To the washing machine

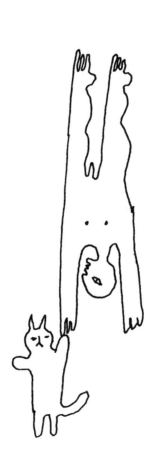

And Of Course, Neither is the Horse

It would be quite reckless
To claim I came from Texas
I'm just a man from Huddersfield
And though we all make mistakes
Don't be fooled I'm just a fake
You've got to understand that I'm not real
And of course
Neither is the horse

It's hard not to be put out
By this cardboard cowboy cut-out
I'm just a country and west riding fool
I've never made my home in
Any places like Wyoming
I've never been further west than Liverpool
And of course
Neither has the horse

It feels strange inside
When you've got no range to ride
And you look like an extra from Wagon Train
But I don't know the answer
'Cos I've never watched *Bonanza*
And I don't want to be John Wayne
And of course
Neither does the horse

Through the wind and snow and hail

I ride this lonesome trail

Misery, mile after mile

'Cos I have searched this whole wide world

Looking for a country girl

'Cos I ain't had no loving for a while

And of course

Neither has the horse

Biscuit

You were some coffee
I was a biscuit
Love dunked me in you
And I fell apart

Wanted; Idlers

I'm looking for people with no sense of direction
To hang around pointlessly with
Please apply PO BOX 17
(no time wasters)

I Left a Small Deposit on a Pair of Trousers

I buy all my clothes from Oxfam
I could go to War on Want or Scope
But I think it's worth paying that little bit extra

Ian Botham

Ian Botham
Ian Botham
Ian Botham

Before a big test match Ian Botham relaxes.
First he drinks twelve pints of Special Brew
With a barley wine in each one

Ian Botham
Ian Botham
Ian Botham

Then he rolls three reefers,
Each one rolled with the *Daily Express*
Involving twelve ounces of Old Holborn
And for the roach he uses the inside of a toilet roll

Ian Botham
Ian Botham
Ian Botham

Then he makes love
Nay, indulges in athletic sexual congress
With divers women
All night

Ian Botham
Ian Botham
Ian Botham

... And then
In the morning he goes out
To face the incredible might
Of the West Indian fast bowlers
And ...
He's out first bowl
Because he's completely smashed
Out of his crust

Ian Botham
Ian Botham
Ian Botham

Yorkshire Song

I was born and bred and buttered
In the north country
And I've often used flat vowels
And sometimes worn flat caps
But I've never heard 'owt like my old man
He'd say, "Ah'll nobbut thraip a leet on t'bugger
If it wain't claht a thradwacker"
And I'd say, "Aye, 'appen, Dad"

I've been from Batley to Bali
I've been from Darlington to Delhi
I've been from Keighley to Khatmandu
But I've never heard 'owt like my old man
He'd say, "'as ta cleamped oer lamp fuss
Or is ta thrappled on t'cleats?"
And I'd say "Aye, 'appen, Dad"

Our Ken is really clever
You can ask him 'owt you like
It doesn't matter if it's astrophysics
Or how to mend your bike
You can ask that bloke anything
He can tell you how and where and when
But when mi Dad speaks broad Yorkshire
It's totally beyond our Ken

Our Ken is my eldest brother
When we were kids we'd play in the woods at Robin Hood.
Because he was my big brother he'd always be Robin
And I'd be Little John or Will Scarlet
(Maid Marion on a bad day)

On my thirteenth birthday our Ken said,

"Look, Rory, it's your birthday

Today, you can be Robin,"

"Wow! That's fantastic," I said

"That's O.K.," he said, "I'll be Batman"

A bit more about the author ...

In his French-speaking persona, Raymond Bizarre, Rory enjoyed a
network radio hit in France with his epic homage to Eric Cantona.
A triumphant accolade for the Englishman abroad, the disc was
played before international matches at the Parc des Princes on
several occasions.

In his lifesize, step-through white horse, Eric, Rory has taken part
in eco-protests, sung songs on TV, gone into schools and even
taken part in a horse show!

But it is as a comedian that Rory Motion is most widely known.
A familiar voice on national radio and local TV, Rory's quirky and
innovative style has endeared him to a wide variety of audiences.
He is equally at home performing at an anarchist benefit as he is
delivering an after-dinner speech for Rotarians.

Rory wishes to acknowledge the presence of a divine power
underwriting his existence, but would like to point out that he
wrote all these poems by himself with no help from anyone.

With thanks to: Mum and Dad (hello?), Matt Harvey, Simon Thackray, Dux,
Tony Allen, Hovis Presley, Lynn and Martin Cavelôt, B&J at the M, Phil Snell,
Nick, Simon, Matthew and Rachael Evans, Nick and Angela, Robert and Lena, Rob
and John (is Bob there?), Mike and Malcolm for being 'The Travelling Libraries',
Alligator Steve, hair by Dettie and of course, Eric the Horse.